THE FABULOUS LOST & FOUND

AND THE LITTLE ROMANIAN MOUSE

WRITTEN BY MARK PALLIS
ILLUSTRATED BY PETER BAYNTON

NEU WESTEND
— PRESS —

For Emily and Lucy. Legends! - MP

For Hannah and Skye - PB

THE FABULOUS LOST & FOUND AND THE LITTLE ROMANIAN MOUSE
Copyright text © 2020 Mark Pallis and Copyright images © 2020 Peter Baynton

All rights reserved. This book or any portion thereof may not be reproduced or used in any manner whatsoever without the express written permission of the publisher except for the use of brief excerpts in a review.

First Printing, 2020
ISBN: 978-1-913595-19-7
NeuWestendPress.com

THE FABULOUS LOST & FOUND

AND THE LITTLE ROMANIAN MOUSE

WRITTEN BY MARK PALLIS
ILLUSTRATED BY PETER BAYNTON

NEU WESTEND
— PRESS —

In the middle of the big city is a tiny yellow building. If anyone loses anything, this is where it ends up.

It is called the Lost and Found.

Mr and Mrs Frog keep everything safe, hoping that someday every lost watch and bag and phone and toy and shoe and cheesegrater will find its owner again.

But the shop is very small. And there are so many lost things. It is all quite a squeeze, but still, it's fabulous.

One sunny day, a little mouse walked in.

"Welcome," said Mrs Frog. "What have you lost?"

"Mi-am pierdut pălăria," said the mouse.

Mr and Mrs Frog could not speak Romanian. They had no idea what the little mouse was saying.

What shall we do? they wondered.

Maybe she's lost an umbrella. Everyone loses an umbrella at least twice, thought Mr Frog.

"Have you lost this?" asked Mr Frog.

"O umbrelă? Nu," replied the mouse.

Then Mrs Frog remembered something that had been handed in a few months ago...

"Is this yours?" Mrs Frog asked, holding up a chunk of cheese.

"Brânză? Nu. Miroase urât!" said the mouse.

"Time to put that cheese in the bin dear," said Mr Frog.

"Maybe the word 'pălărie' means coat," said Mr Frog.

"Now where did I put that nice yellow one?"

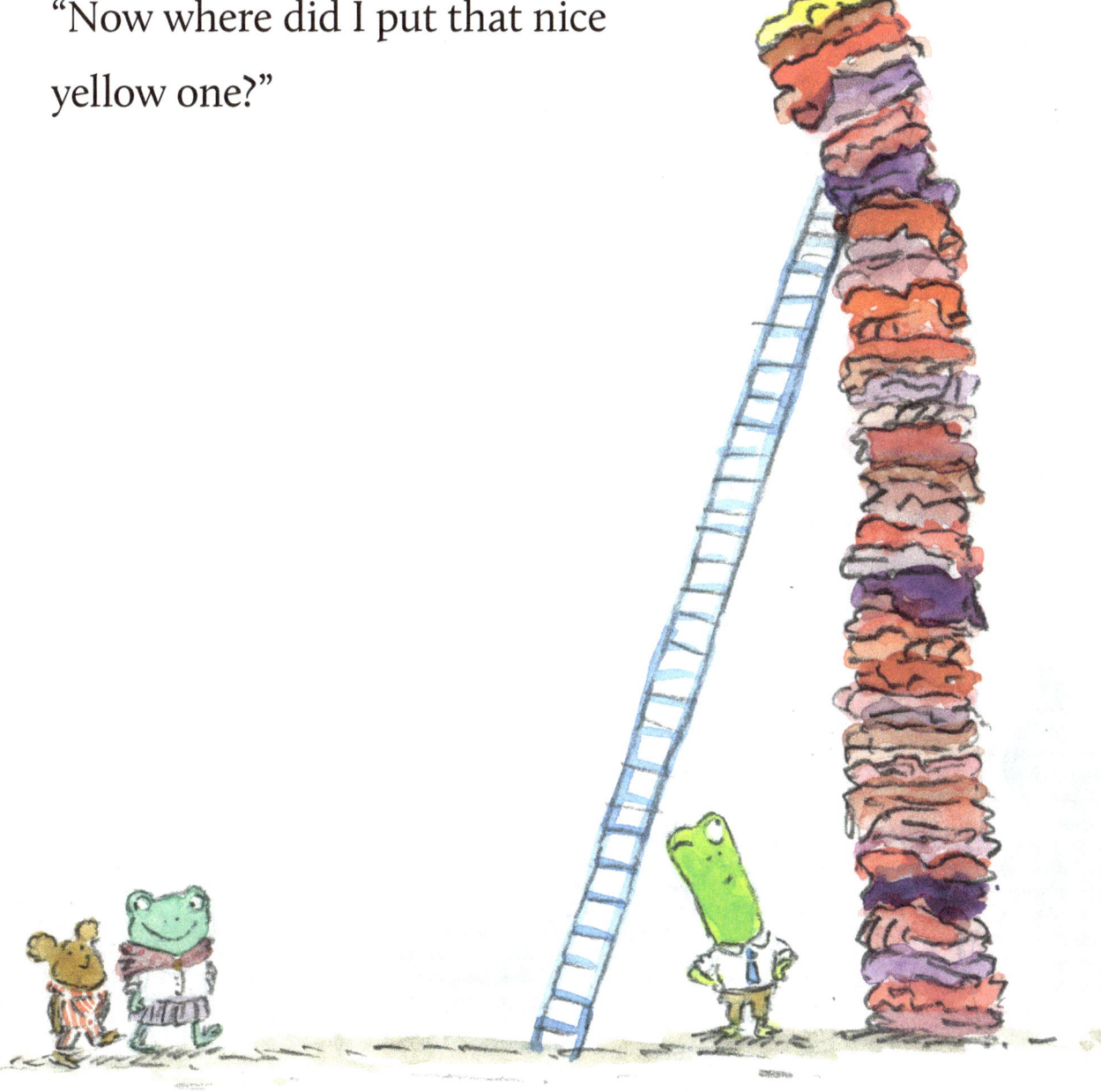

"Got it!" said Mr Frog.

"O haină? Nu. Mi-am pierdut pălăria," said the mouse.

She was starting to feel a bit frustrated.

"We need to keep trying," said Mrs Frog.

Nu o eşarfă.

Nu pantaloni.

Nu pulovăr.

Nu pantofi.

Nu ochelari de soare.

"Mi-am pierdut pălăria," said the mouse.

"How about a nice cup of tea?" asked Mrs Frog kindly.

"Iubesc ceaiul. Mulțumesc," replied the mouse. They sat together, sipping their tea and all feeling a bit sad.

Suddenly, the mouse realised she could try pointing.

She pointed at her head.
"Pălărie!" she said.

"I've got it!" exclaimed Mrs Frog, leaping up.

"A wig of course!" said Mrs Frog.

"Nu o perucă," said the mouse.

Nu roșie.

Nu blondă.

Nu maro.

Nu multicoloră.

Nu verde.

"What about this?" asked Mr Frog, pulling back a curtain.

"Pălărie!" exclaimed the mouse.

"Ah, so 'pălărie' means hat. Wonderful," smiled Mr and Mrs Frog.

Prea înaltă.

Prea mică.

Prea mare.

Prea strâmtă.

"One hat left," said Mrs Frog, reaching all the way to the back of the cupboard.

"It couldn't be this old thing, could it?"

"Pălăria mea.

Mi-am găsit pălăria!

Mulțumesc foarte mult," said the mouse.

And just like that, the mouse found her hat.

"Adio," she said, as she skipped away.
"Adio," replied Mr and Mrs Frog.

"I wonder who will come tomorrow?" said Mr Frog.
Mrs Frog put her arm around him.

"I don't know," she replied, giving him a squeeze,
"but whoever it is, we'll do our best to help."

LEARNING TO LOVE LANGUAGES

An additional language opens a child's mind, broadens their horizons and enriches their emotional life. Research has shown that the time between a child's birth and their sixth or seventh birthday is a "golden period" when they are most receptive to new languages. This is because they have an in-built ability to distinguish the sounds they hear and make sense of them. The Story-powered Language Learning Method taps into these natural abilities.

HOW THE STORY-POWERED LANGUAGE LEARNING METHOD WORKS

We create an emotionally engaging and funny story for children and adults to enjoy together, just like any other picture book. Studies show that social interaction, like enjoying a book together, is critical in language learning.

Through the story, we introduce a relatable character who speaks only in the new language. This helps build empathy and a positive attitude towards people who speak different languages. These are both important aspects in laying the foundations for lasting language acquisition in a child's life.

As the story progresses, the child naturally works with the characters to discover the meaning of a wide range of fun new words. Strategic use of humour ensures that this subconscious learning is rewarded with laughter; the child feels good and the first seeds of a lifelong love of languages are sown.

For more information and free downloads visit www.neuwestendpress.com

ALL THE BEAUTIFUL ROMANIAN WORDS AND PHRASES FROM OUR STORY

mi-am pierdut pălăria	I've lost my hat	*multicolorată*	multicoloured
umbrelă	umbrella	*nu*	no
brânză	cheese	*pălăria mea*	my hat
miroase urât	stinks	*prea înaltă*	too tall
haină	coat	*prea mare*	too big
eșarfă	scarf	*prea mică*	too small
pantaloni	trousers	*prea strâmtă*	too tight
ochelari de soare	sunglasses	*mi-am găsit pălăria*	I've found my hat
pulovăr	sweater	*mulțumesc foarte mult*	thank you very much
pantofi	shoes	*adio*	goodbye
una	one		
două	two		
trei	three		
patru	four		
cinci	five		
computer	computer		
carte	book		
chei	key		
bicicletă	bicycle		
banană	banana		
Iubesc ceaiul	I love tea		
mulțumesc	thanks		
perucă	wig		
roșie	red		
blondă	blond		
maro	brown		
verde	green		

THE WORLD OF
THE FABULOUS LOST & FOUND

THIS STORY IS ALSO AVAILABLE IN...

FRENCH
SPANISH
ITALIAN
CZECH
KOREAN
WELSH
GERMAN
HEBREW
SWEDISH
GREEK
SLOVAKIAN
VIETNAMESE
LATIN
PORTUGUESE

...AND MANY MORE LANGUAGES!

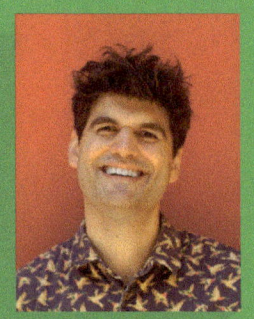

ENJOYED IT?
WRITE A REVIEW AND
LET US KNOW!

@MARK_PALLIS ON TWITTER
WWW.MARKPALLIS.COM

@PETERBAYNTON ON INSTAGRAM
WWW.PETERBAYNTON.COM

www.ingramcontent.com/pod-product-compliance
Lightning Source LLC
Chambersburg PA
CBHW051250110526
44588CB00025B/2940